Warren M. Koontz MD

A MERRY
CHRISTMAS

CHRISTMAS

EDITED BY SHEILA PICKLES

LONDON MCMLXXXIX

For my children
James and Charlotte Rose

and my godchildren
Sarah, Louisa, Tamsin, Rupert,
Alice, Grace and Sarah

and in memory of Rose.

INTRODUCTION

DEAR READER,

Christmas is a time for children and it brings out the child in all of us. It has always been a very special time for me and I still look forward to it and enjoy it tremendously. I suspect this is because Christmas was made into a magical occasion for Susan, my sister, and I as children, and my enthusiasm and enjoyment now stem from creating this magic for others.

When we were small, I remember the excitement starting with writing to Father Christmas and gaining momentum towards Christmas Day, just as D. H. Lawrence describes in *The Rainbow*. Then finally the great day was spent surrounded by parcels and new toys, eating huge meals with visiting relations, and much merriment was had. As I grew up, Christmas Day itself became something of an anticlimax. Perhaps this is because children nowadays have high expectations of Christmas. I know my children would be very disappointed to receive only the one slim volume under their pillows which gave such pleasure to Jo and her sisters in *Little Women*–this is such a sharp contrast to the bonanza which Christmas has become in many homes, and I cannot believe that it is enjoyed any the more for it. On re-reading *A Christmas Carol*, I was struck with guilt at modern expectations of

Christmas and resolved to re-read it each year at the beginning of December to keep Christmas in perspective and spare a thought for those less fortunate than ourselves, like the Cratchits. Interesting too that almost one hundred years ago George Bernard Shaw was rebelling against Christmas for its insincerity and vulgarity. Dickens writes that a man must be a misanthrope if he does not feel some joviality at the recurrence of Christmas and I would say that it is a poor-spirited creature indeed who feels no emotion at hearing the time-worn carols or finding a silver sixpence in his pudding.

It seems to me that with the emphasis there is today on partying and gift-giving, the reasons for celebrating Christmas are often lost and no one says this better than John Betjeman. I feel it is a wonderful opportunity to acknowledge friendships and show appreciation and, of course, spend time with family and friends. Part of the pleasure of Christmas for me is the tradition and familiarity of the rituals: the stirring of the pudding, the decorating of the tree, the filling of the stockings. Seeing the delight on the children's faces makes all the preparation worth while. After the stockings, the ideal Christmas Day continues with Matins, then hearth and home and relaxing with those dear to us. I have dedicated this book to those children who are dear to me in the hope that, as suggested by Elizabeth Bowen, Christmas happiness will always ring out in them like a peal of bells.

Sheila Pickles, Yorkshire 1989

HAPPY, HAPPY CHRISTMAS

CHRISTMAS time! That man must be a misanthrope indeed, in whose breast something like a jovial feeling is not roused – in whose mind some pleasant associations are not awakened – by the recurrence of Christmas. There are people who will tell you that Christmas is not to them what it used to be; that each succeeding Christmas has found some cherished hope, or happy prospect, of the year before, dimmed or passed away; that the present only serves to remind them of reduced circumstances and straitened incomes – of the feasts they once bestowed on hollow friends, and of the cold looks that meet them now, in adversity and misfortune. Never heed such dismal reminiscences. There are few men who have lived long enough in the world, who cannot call up such thoughts any day in the year. Then do not select the merriest of the three hundred and sixty-five for your doleful recollections, but draw your chair nearer the blazing fire – fill the glass and send round the song—and if your room be smaller than it was a dozen years ago, or if your glass be filled with reeking punch, instead of sparkling wine, put a good face on the matter, and empty it off-hand, and fill another, and troll off the old ditty you used to sing, and thank God it's no worse . . .

Who can be insensible to the outpourings of good feeling, and the honest interchange of affectionate attachment which abound at this season of the year. A Christmas family-party! We know nothing in nature more delightful! There seems a magic in the very name of Christmas. Petty jealousies and discords are forgotten; social feelings are awakened, in bosoms to which they have long been strangers; father and son, or brother and sister, who have met and passed with averted gaze, or a look of cold recognition, for months before, proffer and return the cordial embrace, and bury their past animosities in their present happiness. Kindly hearts that have yearned towards each other but have been withheld by false notions of pride and self-dignity, are again reunited, and all is kindness and benevolence! Would that Christmas lasted the whole year through (as it ought) and that the prejudices and passions which deform our better nature were never called into action among those to whom they should ever be strangers!

FROM *SKETCHES BY BOZ* BY CHARLES DICKENS, 1812–1870

CHRISTMAS WAS COMING

GRADUALLY there gathered the feeling of expectation. Christmas was coming. In the shed, at nights, a secret candle was burning, a sound of veiled voices was heard. The boys were learning the old mystery play of St. George and Beelzebub. Twice a week, by lamplight, there was choir practice in the church, for the learning of old carols Brangwen wanted to hear. The girls went to these practices. Everywhere was a sense of mystery and rousedness. Everybody was preparing for something.

The time came near, the girls were decorating the church, with cold fingers binding holly and fir and yew about the pillars, till a new spirit was in the church, the stone broke out into dark, rich leaf, the arches put forth their æuds, and cold flowers rose to blossom in the dim, mystic atmosphere. Ursula must weave mistletoe over the door, and over the screen, and hang a silver dove from a sprig of yew, till dusk came down, and the church was like a grove.

In the cow-shed the boys were blacking their faces for a dress-rehearsal; the turkey hung dead, with opened, speckled wings, in the dairy. The time was come to make pies, in readiness.

The expectation grew more tense. The star was risen into the sky, the songs, the carols were ready to hail it. The star was the sign in the sky. Earth too should give a sign. As evening drew on, hearts beat fast with anticipation, hands were full of ready gifts. There were the tremulously expectant words of the church service, the night was past and the morning was come, the gifts were given and received, joy and peace made a flapping of wings in each heart, there was a great burst of carols, the Peace of the World had dawned, strife had passed away, every hand was linked in hand, every heart was singing.

FROM *THE RAINBOW* BY D. H. LAWRENCE, 1885–1930

Good Christian Men, Rejoice

ood Christian men, rejoice
With heart and soul and voice!
Now ye hear of endless bliss:
Joy! Joy!
Jesus Christ was born for this.
He hath oped the heavenly door,
And man is blest for evermore.
Christ was born for this.

John Mason Neale, 1818–1866

A SEASONABLE SIGHT

AT last the Rat succeeded in decoying him to the table, and had just got seriously to work with the sardine-opener when sounds were heard from the fore-court without–sounds like the scuffling of small feet in the gravel and a confused murmur of tiny voices, while broken sentences reached them–"Now, all in a line–hold the lantern up a bit, Tommy–clear your throats first–no coughing after I say one, two three.–Where's young Bill?–Here, come on, do, we're all a-waiting——"

"What's up?" inquired the Rat, pausing in his labours.

"I think it must be the field-mice," replied the Mole, with a touch of pride in his manner. "They go round carol-singing regularly at this time of the year. They're quite an institution in these parts. And they never pass me over–they come to Mole End last of all; and I used to give them hot drinks, and supper too sometimes, when I could afford it. It will be like old times to hear them again."

"Let's have a look at them!" cried the Rat, jumping up and running to the door.

It was a pretty sight, and a seasonable one, that met their eyes when they flung the door open. In the fore-court, lit by the dim rays of a horn lantern, some eight or ten little field-mice stood in a semi-circle, red worsted comforters round their throats, their fore-paws thrust deep into their pockets, their feet jigging for warmth. With bright beady eyes they glanced shyly at each other, sniggering a little, sniffing and applying coat-sleeves a good deal. As the door opened, one of the older ones that carried the lantern was just saying, "Now then, one, two, three!" and forthwith their shrill little voices uprose on the air, singing one of the old-time carols that their forefathers composed in fields that were fallow and held by frost, or when snow-bound in chimney corners, and handed down to be sung in the miry street to lamp-lit windows at Yule-time.

FROM *THE WIND IN THE WILLOWS* BY KENNETH GRAHAME, 1859–1932

THE HOLLY AND THE IVY

THE Holly and the Ivy,
When they are both full grown
Of all the trees are in the wood,
The Holly bears the crown.

The Holly bears a blossom
As white as any flower;
And Mary bore sweet Jesus Christ
To be our sweet Saviour.

The Holly bears a berry
As red as any blood;
And Mary bore sweet Jesus Christ
To do poor sinners good.

The Holly bears a prickle
As sharp as any thorn;
And Mary bore sweet Jesus Christ
On Christmas in the morn.

The Holly bears a bark
As bitter as any gall;
And Mary bore sweet Jesus Christ
For to redeem us all.

The Holly and the Ivy
Now both are full well grown:
Of all the trees are in the wood
The Holly bears the crown.

FIFTEENTH-CENTURY ENGLISH CAROL

DECEMBER CHRISTMAS

Christmass is come and every hearth
Makes room to give him welcome now
Een want will dry its tears in mirth
And crown him wi a holly bough
Tho tramping neath a winters sky
Oer snow track paths and ryhmey stiles
The huswife sets her spining bye
And bids him welcome wi her smiles

Neighbours resume their anual cheer
Wishing wi smiles and spirits high
Glad christmass and a happy year
To every morning passer bye
Milk maids their christmass journeys go
Accompanyd wi favourd swain
And childern pace the crumping snow
To taste their grannys cake again.

FROM *THE SHEPHERD'S CALENDAR*
BY JOHN CLARKE, 1609–1676

CHRISTMAS

The bells of waiting Advent ring,
The Tortoise stove is lit again
And lamp-oil light across the night
Has caught the streaks of winter rain
In many a stained-glass window sheen
From Crimson Lake to Hooker's Green.

The holly in the windy hedge
And round the Manor House the yew
Will soon be stripped to deck the ledge,
The altar, font and arch and pew,
So that the villagers can say
"The church looks nice" on Christmas Day.

Provincial public houses blaze
And Corporation tramcars clang,
On lighted tenements I gaze
Where paper decorations hang,
And bunting in the red Town Hall
Says "Merry Christmas to you all"

And London shops on Christmas Eve
   Are strung with silver bells and flowers
As hurrying clerks the City leave
   To pigeon-haunted classic towers,
And marbled clouds go scudding by
The many-steepled London sky.

And girls in slacks remember Dad,
   And oafish louts remember Mum,
And sleepless children's hearts are glad,
   And Christmas-morning bells say "Come!"
Even to shining ones who dwell
Safe in the Dorchester Hotel.

And is it true? And is it true,
   This most tremendous tale of all,
Seen in a stained-glass window's hue,
   A Baby in an ox's stall?
The Maker of the stars and sea
Become a Child on earth for me?

And is it true? For if it is,
   No loving fingers tying strings
Around those tissued fripperies,
   The sweet and silly Christmas things,
Bath salts and inexpensive scent
And hideous tie so kindly meant,

No love that in a family dwells,
   No carolling in frosty air,
Nor all the steeple-shaking bells
   Can with this single Truth compare-
That God was Man in Palestine
And lives to-day in Bread and Wine.

JOHN BETJEMAN, 1906–1984

Christmas in Olden Time

The fire, with well-dried logs supplied,
Went roaring up the chimney wide;
The huge hall-table's oaken face,
Scrubb'd till it shone, the day to grace,
Bore then upon its massive board
No mark to part the squire and lord.
Then was brought in the lusty brawn,
By old blue-coated serving-man;
Then the grim boar's head frown'd on high,
Crested with bays and rosemary.
Well can the green-garb'd ranger tell,
How, when, and where, the monster fell;
What dogs before his death he tore,
And all the baiting of the boar.
The wassel round, in good brown bowls,
Garnish'd with ribbons, blithely trowls.
There the huge sirloin reek'd; hard by
Plum-porridge stood, and Christmas pie;
Nor fail'd old Scotland to produce,
At such high tide, her savoury goose.
Then come the merry maskers in,
And carols roar'd with blithesome din;
If unmelodious was the song,
It was hearty note, and strong.
Who lists may in their mumming see
Traces of ancient mystery;
White shirts supplied the masquerade,
And smutted cheeks the visors made;
But, O! what maskers, richly dight,
Can boast of bosoms half so light!
England was merry England, when
Old Christmas brought his sports again.
'Twas Christmas broach'd the mightiest ale;
'Twas Christmas told the merriest tale;
A Christmas gambol oft could cheer
The poor man's heart through half the year.

Sir Walter Scott, 1771–1832

A Hansom Cab

Naturally Tony wanted to see the shops, and as soon as the Christmas holidays began I was allowed to go with her and mother to the West End. Tony was all for taking hansoms. As she pointed out, a bus can be taken any day – a holiday was a holiday, and she didn't believe in doing things by halves. She argued that it is the regular expenses that one should worry about, not the occasional. So she took hansoms right and left, and I can still recall the luxurious feeling of snuggling down in a hansom between her and mother, to be wafted exactly where we wanted to go. I could just see the toss of the horse's head and could hear the klip-klop of his hoofs and the cheerful jingle of his bells. It is amusing to reflect now that the bells on a hansom were put there as a warning to pedestrians to get out of the way of such swift vehicles. Those were the days when a man with a red flag used to walk in front of a steam-roller. I wonder what Tony would say to the traffic in Piccadilly to-day. On one of her later visits to London I took her on the top of a bus, to see some of the life of the town. As I called her attention to this and that, she said, "Don't ask me to look, dear. If I take my eye off the driver he will surely run into something."

From *A London Child of the 1870s* by M. V. Hughes, 1866–1956

A COUNTRY PARSON'S CHRISTMAS EVE

WRITING Christmas letters all the morning. In the afternoon I went to the church with Dora and Teddy to put up Christmas decorations. Dora had been very busy for some days past making the straw letters for the Christmas text. Fair Rosamund and good Elizabeth Knight came to the church to help us and worked heartily and well. They had made some pretty ivy knots and bunches for the pulpit panels and the ivy blossoms cleverly whitened with flour looked just like white flowers.

The churchwarden Jacob Knight was sitting by his sister in front of the roaring fire. We were talking of the death of Major Torrens on the ice at Corsham pond yesterday. Speaking of people slipping and falling on ice the good churchwarden sagely remarked, "Some do fall on their faces and some do fall on their rumps. And they as do hold their selves uncommon stiff do most in generally fall on their rumps."

I took old John Bryant a Christmas packet of tea and sugar and raisins from my Mother. The old man had covered himself almost entirely over in his bed to keep himself warm, like a marmot in its nest. He said, "If I live till New Year's Day I shall have seen ninety-six New Years." He said also, "I do often see things flying about me, thousands and thousands of them about half the size of a large pea, and they are red, white, blue, and yellow and all colours. I asked Mr Morgan what they were and he said they were the spirits of just men made perfect."

FROM *DIARY 1870–1879* BY THE REV. FRANCIS KILVERT

THE OXEN

CHRISTMAS Eve, and twelve of the clock.
"Now they are all on their knees,"
An elder said as we sat in a flock
By the embers in hearthside ease.

We pictured the meek mild creatures where
They dwelt in their strawy pen,
Nor did it occur to one of us there
To doubt they were kneeling then.

So fair a fancy few would weave
In these years! Yet, I feel,
If someone said on Christmas Eve,
"Come; see the oxen kneel

"In the lonely barton by yonder coomb
Our childhood used to know,"
I should go with him in the gloom,
Hoping it might be so.

THOMAS HARDY, 1840–1928

A Visit from St Nicholas

Down the chimney St. Nicholas came with a bound.
He was dressed all in fur from his head to his foot,
And his clothes were all tarnished with ashes and soot;
A bundle of toys he had flung on his back,
And he looked like a peddler just opening his pack.
His eyes how they twinkled! his dimples how merry!
His cheeks were like roses, his nose like a cherry;
His droll little mouth was drawn up like a bow,
And the beard on his chin was as white as the snow.
The stump of a pipe he held tight in his teeth,
And the smoke it encircled his head like a wreath.
He had a broad face, and a little round belly
That shook, when he laughed, like a bowl full of jelly.
He was chubby and plump,—a right jolly old elf—
And I laughed when I saw him, in spite of myself.
A wink of his eye and a twist of his head
Soon gave me to know I had nothing to dread.
He spoke not a word, but went straight to his work,
And filled all the stockings; then turned with a jerk,
And laying his finger aside of his nose,
And giving a nod, up the chimney he rose.
He sprang to his sleigh, to his team gave a whistle,
And away they all flew like the down of a thistle;
But I heard him exclaim, ere he drove out of sight:
"Happy Christmas to all, and to all a good-night!"

Clement Clarke Moore, 1779–1863

Small Boy. And then the Presents?

Self. And then the Presents, after the Christmas box. And the cold postman, with a rose on his button-nose, tingled down the teatray-slithered run of the chilly glinting hill. He went in his ice-bound boots like a man on fishmonger's slabs. He wagged his bag like a frozen camel's hump, dizzily turned the corner on one foot, and, by God, he was gone.

Small Boy. Get back to the Presents.

Self. There were the Useful Presents: engulfing mufflers of the old coach days, and mittens made for giant sloths; zebra scarves of a substance like silky gum that could be tug-o'-warred down to the goloshes; blinding tam-O'-shanters like patchwork tea-cosies, and bunnys-cutted busbies and balaclavas for victims of head-shrinking tribes; from aunts who always wore wool-next-to-the-skin, there were moustached and rasping vests that made you wonder why the aunties had any skin left at all; and once I had a little crocheted nose-bag from an aunt now, alas, no longer whinnying with us. And pictureless books in which small boys, though warned, with quotations, not to, *would* skate on Farmer Garge's pond, and did, and drowned; and books that told me everything about the wasp, except why.

Small Boy. Get on to the Useless Presents.

Self. On Christmas Eve I hung at the foot of my bed Bessie Bunter's black stocking, and always, I said, I would stay awake all the moonlit, snowlit night to hear the roof-alighting reindeer and see the hollied boot descend through soot. But soon the sand of the snow drifted into my eyes, and, though I stared towards the fireplace and around the flickering room where the black sack-like stocking hung, I was asleep before the chimney trembled and the room was red and white with Christmas. But in

the morning, though no snow melted on the bedroom floor, the stocking bulged and brimmed; press it, it squeaked like a mouse-in-a-box; it smelt of tangerine; a furry arm lolled over, like the arm of a kangaroo out of its mother's belly; squeeze it hard in the middle, and something squelched; squeeze it again–squelch again. Look out of the frost-scribbled window: on the great loneliness of the small hill, a blackbird was silent in the snow.

Small Boy. Were there any sweets?

Self. Of course there were sweets. It was the marshmallows that squelched. Hardboileds, toffee, fudge and allsorts, crunches, cracknels, humbugs, glaciers, and marzipan and butterwelsh for the Welsh. And troops of bright tin soldiers who, if they would not fight, could always run. And Snakes-and-Families and Happy Ladders. And Easy Hobbi-Games for Little Engineers, complete with Instructions. Oh, easy for Leonardo! And a whistle to make the dogs bark to wake up the old man next door to make him beat on the wall with his stick to shake our picture off the wall. And a packet of cigarettes: you put one in your mouth and you stood at the corner of the street and you waited for hours, in vain, for an old lady to scold you for smoking a cigarette and then, with a smirk, you ate it. And, last of all, in the toe of the stocking, sixpence like a silver corn. And then downstairs for breakfast under the balloons!

FROM *A PROSPECT OF THE SEA*
BY DYLAN THOMAS, 1914–1953

CHRISTMAS MORNING

Jo was the first to wake in the gray dawn of Christmas morning. No stockings hung at the fireplace, and for a moment she felt as much disappointed as she did long ago, when her little sock fell down because it was so crammed with goodies. Then she remembered her mother's promise, and slipping her hand under her pillow, drew out a little crimson-covered book. She knew it very well, for it was that beautiful old story of the best life ever lived, and Jo felt that it was a true guide-book for any pilgrim going the long journey. She woke Meg with a "Merry Christmas," and bade her see what was under her pillow. A green-covered book appeared, with the same picture inside, and a few words written by their mother, which made their one present very precious in their eyes. Presently Beth and Amy woke, to rummage and find their little books also,—one dove-colored, the other blue; and all sat looking at and talking about them, while the east grew rosy with the coming day.

FROM *LITTLE WOMEN* BY LOUISA MAY ALCOTT, 1832–1888

GLOUCESTERSHIRE WASSAIL

ASSAIL, Wassail, all over the town!
Our toast it is white, and our ale it is brown,
Our bowl it is made of the white maple tree;
With the wassailing bowl we'll drink to thee.

And here is to Dobbin and to his right eye,
Pray God send our master a good Christmas pie,
And a good Christmas pie that may we all see;
With our wassailing bowl we'll drink to thee . . .

TRADITIONAL

GOD BLESS US EVERY ONE

HALLO! A great deal of steam! The pudding was out of the copper. A smell like a washing-day! That was the cloth. A smell like an eating-house and a pastrycook's next door to each other, with a laundress's next door to that! That was the pudding! In half a minute Mrs Cratchit entered – flushed, but smiling proudly – with the pudding, like a speckled cannon-ball, so hard and firm, blazing in half of half-a-quartern of ignited brandy, and bedight with Christmas holly stuck into the top.

Oh, a wonderful pudding! Bob Cratchit said, and calmly too, that he regarded it as the greatest success achieved by Mrs Cratchit since their marriage. Mrs Cratchit said that now the weight was off her mind, she would confess she had had her doubts about the quantity of flour. Everybody had something to say about it, but nobody said or thought it was at all a small pudding for a large family. It would have been flat heresy to do so. Any Cratchit would have blushed to hint at such a thing.

At last the dinner was all done, the cloth was cleared, the hearth swept, and the fire made up. The compound in the jug being tasted, and considered perfect, apples and oranges were put upon the table, and a shovel-full of chestnuts on the fire. Then all the Cratchit family drew round the hearth, in what Bob Cratchit called a circle, meaning half a one; and at Bob Cratchit's elbow stood the family display of glass. Two tumblers, and a custard-cup without a handle.

These held the hot stuff from the jug, however, as well as golden goblets would have done; and Bob served it out with beaming looks, while the chestnuts on the fire sputtered and cracked noisily. Then Bob proposed:

"A Merry Christmas to us all, my dears. God bless us!"

Which all the family re-echoed.

"God bless us every one!" said Tiny Tim, the last of all.

FROM *A CHRISTMAS CAROL* BY CHARLES DICKENS, 1812–1870

A CHRISTMAS TREE

I HAVE been looking on, this evening, at a merry company of children assembled round that pretty German toy, a Christmas Tree. The tree was planted in the middle of a great round table, and towered high above their heads. It was brilliantly lighted by a multitude of little tapers; and everywhere sparkled and glittered with bright objects. There were rosy-cheeked dolls, hiding behind the green leaves; and there were real watches (with movable hands, at least, and an endless capacity of being wound up) dangling from innumerable twigs; there were French-polished tables, chairs, bedsteads, wardrobes, eight-day clocks, and various other articles of domestic furniture (wonderfully made, in tin, at Wolverhampton), perched among the boughs, as if in preparation for some fairy housekeeping; there were jolly, broad-faced little men, much more agreeable in appearance than many real men—and no wonder, for their heads took off, and showed them to be full of sugar-plums; there were fiddles and drums; there were tambourines, books, work-boxes, paint-boxes, sweetmeat boxes, peep-show boxes, and all kinds of boxes; there were trinkets for the elder girls, far brighter than any grown-up gold and jewels; there were baskets and pincushions in all devices; there were guns, swords, and banners; there were witches standing in enchanted rings of pasteboard, to tell fortunes; there were teetotums, humming-tops, needle-cases, pen-wipers, smelling-bottles, conversation-cards, bouquet-holders; real fruit, made artificially dazzling with gold leaf; imitation apples, pears, and walnuts, crammed with surprises; in short, as a pretty child, before me, delightedly whispered to another pretty child, her bosom friend, "There was everything, and more."

FROM *CHRISTMAS STORIES* BY CHARLES DICKENS, 1812–1870

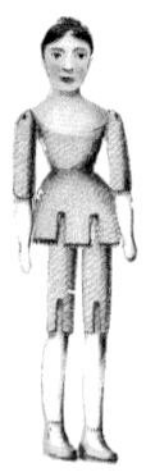

OUR CHRISTMAS AT HOME

WE had been very merry all day, and, as soon as the lights were brought in at tea-time, we came trooping into the parlour from all parts of the house–some from the dairy, where Mary had been making butter; others from the nursery, where they had been playing at soldiers; and the rest from the apple-store over the stable and the school-room, then used only as a play-room, it being holiday time.

We were all assembled in the parlour, and, after tea, my mother told us that we might have a game at romps. We needed no second bidding, and so to play we went in good earnest. We played at Hunt the Slipper and Forfeits, and I don't know how many other games, till we were called into the kitchen for a dance. A good old country dance it was, in which the family, servants, and all joined, noisily enough–all but my mother, who sat under a sort of arbour of holly and other green leaves–for there were always plenty of green leaves and red berries to be got in the garden and orchard, however severe the winter might be–and encouraged us with kind words and beaming smiles. After we were tired of dancing–which was not soon, I assure you–a great china bowl of raisins was brought in by John the butler, who acted occasionally as gardener and coachman as well, and was, in fact, a sort of Jack-of-all-trades. What fun there was, to be sure as we ran dancing and singing round the lighted bowl, snatching the plums from the blue flames of the burning spirit, till they were all gone and the blue flames burned

themselves out. Well, Snap-dragon over, we had kisses under the Mistletoe; and I recollect quite well how we all laughed when Papa took Betty the cook under the white-berried bough and gave her a great loud kiss.

But our fun had not yet ended. At a signal from my mother we followed her into the dining-room on the other side of the passage. Here a sight awaited us that surprised us one and all. The room was brilliantly lighted up with wax candles on sconces from the walls; and on the table in the centre there was placed a great Christmas Tree, hung all over with little lamps and bon-bons, and toys and sweetmeats and bags of cakes. It was the first tree of the kind that I and my companions had ever seen. It was quite a new-fashion the Christmas Tree; and my brother Tom, who had just come home from Germany, had superintended its getting up and decoration. With what shouts of joy we hailed the pretty Christmas Tree, and with what glee and laughter we began to search among its twinkling lights and bright green leaves for the toys and sweetmeats that were hanging there, each one with a name written on its envelope, I can hardly tell you. But we were very merry, I know, and very grateful to our dear mother for her care in providing this delightful surprise as a finish to our merry evening's sports.

ANONYMOUS, *THE CHRISTMAS TREE*, 1857

Blind Man's Buff

We shall have sport when Christmas comes,
When "snap-dragon" burns our fingers and thumbs:
We'll hang mistletoe over our dear little cousins,
And pull them beneath it and kiss them by dozens:
We shall have games at "Blind Man's Buff,"
And noise and laughter and romping enough.

We'll crown the plum-pudding with bunches of bay,
And roast all the chestnuts that come in our way;
And when Twelfth Night falls, we'll have such a cake
That as we stand round it the table shall quake.
We'll draw "King and Queen," and be happy together,
And dance old "Sir Roger" with hearts like a feather.
Home for the Holidays, here we go!
But this Fast train is really exceedingly slow!

Home for the Holidays, Anonymous

CHRISTMAS DAY AT SEA

In all my twenty years of wandering over the restless waters of the globe I can only remember one Christmas Day celebrated by a present given and received. It was, in my view, a proper live-sea transaction, no offering of Dead Sea fruit; and in its unexpectedness perhaps worth recording....

The daybreak of Christmas Day in the year 1879 was fine. The sun began to shine sometime about four o'clock over the somber expanse of the Southern Ocean in latitude 51; and shortly afterwards a sail was sighted ahead. The wind was light, but a heavy swell was running. Presently I wished a "Merry Christmas" to my captain. He looked sleepy, but amiable. I reported the distant sail to him and ventured the opinion that there was something wrong with her. He said, "Wrong?" in an incredulous tone. I pointed out that she had all her upper sails furled and that she was brought to the wind, which, in that region of the world, could not be accounted for on any other theory....

The captain, as is a captain's way, disappeared from the deck; and after a time our carpenter came up the poop ladder carrying an empty small wooden keg, of the sort in which certain ship's provisions are packed. I said, surprised, "What do you mean by lugging this thing up here, Chips?"

"Captain's orders, sir," he explained shortly.

I did not like to question him further, and so we only exchanged Christmas greetings and he went away. The next person to speak to me was the steward. He came running up the companion stairs. "Have you any old newspapers in your room, sir?"

We had left Sydney, N.S.W., eighteen days before. There were several old Sydney *Heralds*, *Telegraphs*, *Bulletins* in my cabin, besides a few home papers received by the last mail. "Why do you ask, steward?" I inquired naturally.

"The captain would like to have them," he said.

And even then I did not understand the inwardness of these eccentricities. I was only lost in astonishment at them. It was eight o'clock before we had closed with that ship, which, under her short canvas and heading nowhere in particular, seemed to be loafing aimlessly on the very threshold of the gloomy home of storms. But long before that hour I learned from the number of boats she carried that this nonchalant ship was a whaler. She had hoisted the Stars and Stripes at her peak, and her signal flags had already told us that her name was *Alaska*–two years out from New York–east from Honolulu–two hundred and fifteen days on the cruising ground.

We passed, sailing slowly, within a hundred yards of her; and just as our steward started ringing the breakfast bell, the captain and I held aloft, in good view of the figures watching us over her stern, the keg, properly headed up and containing, besides an enormous bundle of newspapers, two boxes of figs in honor of the day. We flung it far out over the rail. Instantly our ship, sliding down the slope of a high swell, left it far behind in our wake. On board the *Alaska* a man in a fur cap flourished an arm; another, a much bewhiskered person, ran forward suddenly. I never saw anything so ready and so smart as the way that whaler, rolling desperately all the time, lowered one of her boats. The Southern Ocean went on tossing the two ships like a juggler his gilt balls, and the microscopic white speck of the boat seemed to come into the game instantly, as if shot out from a catapult on the enormous and lonely stage. That Yankee whaler lost not a moment in picking up her Christmas present from the English wool clipper.

FROM *CHRISTMAS DAY AT SEA* BY JOSEPH CONRAD, 1857–1924

AN ATROCIOUS INSTITUTION

The World, 20 December 1893

LIKE all intelligent people, I greatly dislike Christmas. It revolts me to see a whole nation refrain from music for weeks together in order that every man may rifle his neighbour's pockets under cover of a ghastly general pretence of festivity. It is really an atrocious institution, this Christmas. We must be gluttonous because it is Christmas. We must be drunken because it is Christmas. We must be insincerely generous; we must buy things that nobody wants, and give them to people we don't like; we must go to absurd entertainments that make even our little children satirical; we must writhe under venal officiousness from legions of freebooters, all because it is Christmas–that is, because the mass of the population, including the all-powerful middle-class tradesman, depends on a week of licence and brigandage, waste and intemperance, to clear off its outstanding liabilities at the end of the year.

GEORGE BERNARD SHAW, 1856–1950

benedicent te glori
am regni tui dicent

Alleluya.

O Little Town of Bethlehem

O little town of Bethlehem,
How still we see thee lie!
Above thy deep and dreamless sleep
The silent stars go by:
Yet in thy dark street shineth
The everlasting Light;
The hopes and fears of all the years
Are met in thee to-night.

O morning stars, together
Proclaim the holy birth,
And praises sing to God the King,
And peace to men on earth;
For Christ is born of Mary;
And, gathered all above,
While mortals sleep, the angels keep
Their watch of wondering love.

PHILLIPS BROOKS, 1835–1893

HOME FOR CHRISTMAS

THIS is meeting time again. Home is the magnet. The winter land roars and hums with the eager speed of return journeys. The dark is noisy and bright with late-night arrivals—doors thrown open, running shadows on snow, open arms, kisses, voices and laughter, laughter at everything and nothing. Inarticulate, giddying and confused are those original minutes of being back again. The very familiarity of everything acts like shock. Contentment has to be drawn in slowly, steadyingly, in deep breaths—there is so much of it. We rely on home not to change, and it does not, wherefore we give thanks. Again Christmas: abiding point of return. Set apart by its mystery, mood and magic, the season seems in a way to stand outside time. All that is dear, that is lasting, renews its hold on us: we are home again. . . .

FROM *HOME FOR CHRISTMAS* BY ELIZABETH BOWEN, 1899–1973

Text Acknowledgements

'Christmas' © John Betjeman, Curtis Brown Ltd; Extract from 'A London Child of the 1870s' by M V Hughes, 1934, Oxford University Press; Extract from 'A Prospect of the Sea' from *The Collected Stories of Dylan Thomas*, J M Dent & Sons, London, USA: New Directions Publishing Corporation; Extract from 'Shaw's Music', Society of Authors/Bernard Shaw Estate; 'Home for Christmas' © 1957, Elizabeth Bowen, Prentice-Hall Inc., Curtis Brown Ltd.

Picture Acknowledgements

In order of appearance

Anon, Bridgeman Art Library; Anon, Fine Art Photographic Library; George Sheridan Knowles, Fine Art Photographic; Rosina Emmett, E T Archive, Victoria & Albert Museum; Anon, Fine Art Photographic Library; Gerald Portielje, Bridgeman Art Library; Anon, Bridgeman Art Library; Walter Dendy Sadler, Bridgeman Art Library; Augustus E Mulready, Fine Art Photographic Library; William M Spittle, Fine Art Photographic Library; Lizzie Mack, Mary Evans Picture Library; John Callcott Horsley RA, Fine Art Photographic Library; Frederick Marianus Kruseman, Fine Art Photographic Library; Anon, Fine Art Photographic Library; Petrus van Schendel, Christies, Bridgeman Art Library; W Ashwood, Fine Art Photographic Library; Anon, Fine Art Photographic Library; Sir Henry Raeburn, Bridgeman Art Library; Sandro Bottecelli (detail), Bridgeman Art Library; Adolf Eberle, Bridgeman Art Library; Anon, Fine Art Photographic Library; Anon, Fine Art Photographic Library; Otto Haslund, Fine Art Photographic Library; Anon, Bridgeman Art Library; Carl-Christian, Bridgeman Art Library; Walter Dendy Sadler, Fine Art Photographic Library; Anon, Fine Art Photographic Library; Albert Chavalier Taylor, Bridgeman Art Library; Albert Chavalier Taylor, Bridgeman Art Library; Viggo Johansen, Bridgeman Art Library; Anon, Mary Evans Picture Library; St Clair Simmonds, Mary Evans Picture Library; William Small, Bridgeman Art Library; Anon, Bridgeman Art Library; Dante Gabriel Rossetti, Delaware Art Museum; Thomas Gotch, Tate Gallery; Charles Theodore Frere, Fine Art Photographic Library; Antonio Correggio, Bridgeman Art Library; John Ritchie, Fine Art Photographic Library; Anon, Fine Art Photographic Library; Jules Emile Saintin, Bridgeman Art Library.

Jacket: *Happy Christmas* by Viggo Johansen, Hirsch Sprungske Collection, Copenhagen, Bridgeman Art Library.

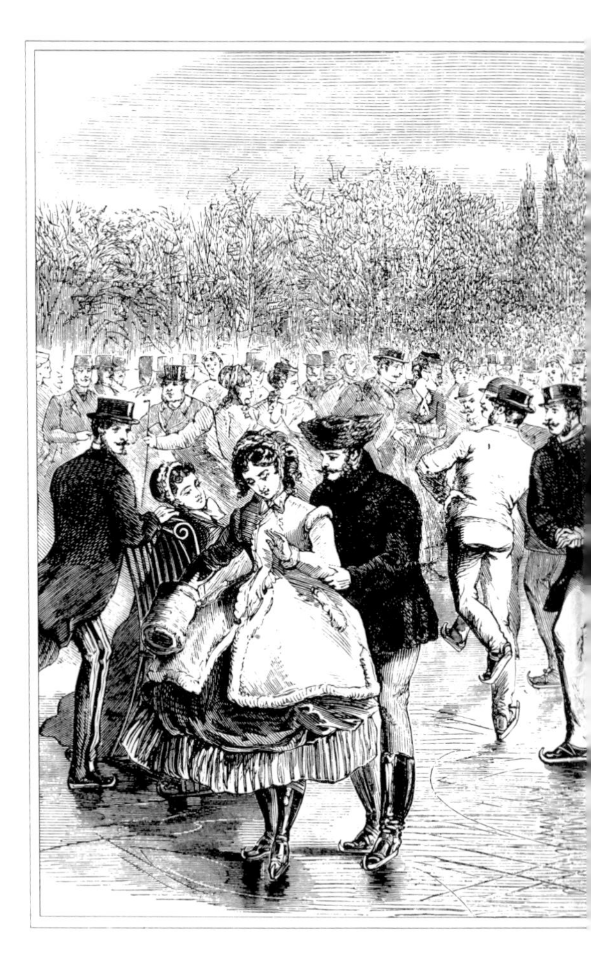

PENHALIGON'S
AT HOME
THE WINTER GARDEN

PENHALIGON'S Book of Christmas is scented with The Winter Garden which we introduced for Christmas last year. We developed it especially for use in the Autumn and Winter when the garden is no longer producing fragrant blossoms for use indoors. With its spicy notes of cloves and cinnamon and small fir cones, it is reminiscent of hot toddies and log fires and guaranteed to add a festive air.

Published in the United States by Harmony Books, a division of Crown Publishers, Inc., 201 East 50th Street, New York, New York, 10022. Member of the Crown Publishing Group.

Published in Great Britain by Pavilion Books Limited

Random House, Inc. New York, Toronto, London, Sydney, Auckland

HARMONY and colphon are trademarks of Crown Publishers, Inc.

Manufactured in China by Imago

Design by Bernard Higton

Library of Congress Catalog Card Number: 89-1906

ISBN 0-517-59900-7

10 9 8 7 6 5 4 3 2